SOUTHEAST ENTRANCE   *Photo by Daniel Stern*

© 2004 Botanical Garden Foundation, Inc.
ISBN 0-9744370-0-x

Library of Congress Catalog Number 2004091826

Stern, Daniel.
A Haven in the Heart of Chapel Hill

Printed in the USA

A Haven in the Heart of Chapel Hill

Artists Celebrate the Coker Arboretum

BY

Daniel Stern

BOTANICAL GARDEN FOUNDATION
CHAPEL HILL, NORTH CAROLINA

ACKNOWLEDGMENTS

*The Coker Arboretum and the Botanical Garden Foundation would like to thank
each of the artists listed below who graciously gave their time and talent
to create the artwork for this book.*

Natalie Crawford
Kristen Dill
Beverly Dixon
Margaret Brunson Hill
Tama Hochbaum
Marriott Little
Jennifer Miller
Pamela Pease
Katherine Shelburne
Emma Skurnick
Barb Spang
Sally Sutton
Dorothy Wilbur-Brooks
Patricia Young

Text by Daniel Stern
Edited by Sandra Brooks-Mathers
Book design by Pamela Pease

*We gratefully acknowledge Diane Birkemo, Sandra Brooks-Mathers, Rob Gardner, J. Horton, Morgan Kenney,
Jim Massey, T.A. Redmon, Daniel Stern, Dorothy Wilbur-Brooks, and Ben and Margaret Williams for their
various and invaluable contributions to this collaboration.*

*We also send appreciation to the Chapel Hill Museum, the UNC General Alumni Association, and the UNC
Press for contributing additional images and words to enrich the pages of this book. The project could not
have happened without the leadership of Nancy Preston, who, along with Arthur DeBerry, Anne Lindsey,
Harriet Martin, and Betsy Pringle, worked diligently to make a book from art, text, and imagination.*

ALL PROCEEDS FROM BOOK SALES WILL SUPPORT THE COKER ARBORETUM ENDOWMENT,
THEREBY ENSURING THE PROPER CARE OF THE ARBORETUM FOR YEARS TO COME.

W*elcome to the Coker Arboretum, the oldest part of the North Carolina Botanical Garden at the University of North Carolina in Chapel Hill. The Arboretum is located on the corner of Cameron Avenue and Raleigh Street in the heart of the University's campus, about two blocks from downtown Chapel Hill.*

This book is written as though you were taking a walking tour of the Coker Arboretum. I hope that the feeling of sanctuary which we have tried to capture on these pages inspires you to reflect on the vision of those who began creating this garden over a century ago and the importance of preserving it for generations to come.

The map following the title page depicts the Arboretum and its immediate surroundings, and the numbers on the overlay correspond to plates of original artwork in order of appearance.

For those of you who are reading A Haven in the Heart of Chapel Hill *from a place far away from the Arboretum, I hope that the artists' renderings and text will bring you some of the pleasures of this very special garden.*

Daniel Stern
Curator, Coker Arboretum
Chapel Hill, North Carolina
April 2004

Artistically embellished aerial photograph courtesy of the Chapel Hill Museum

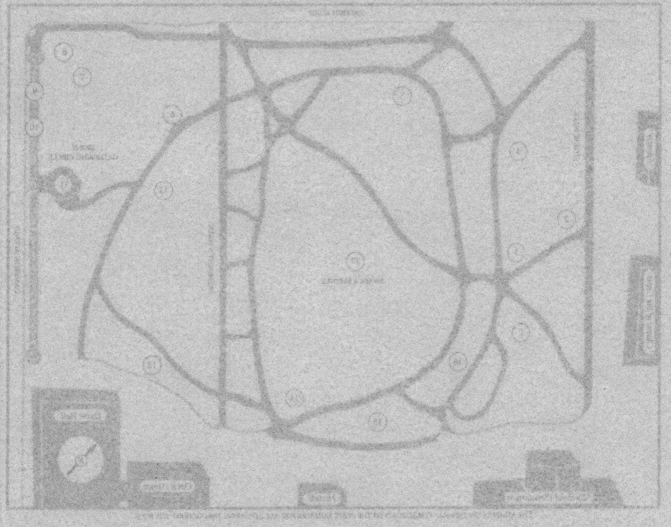

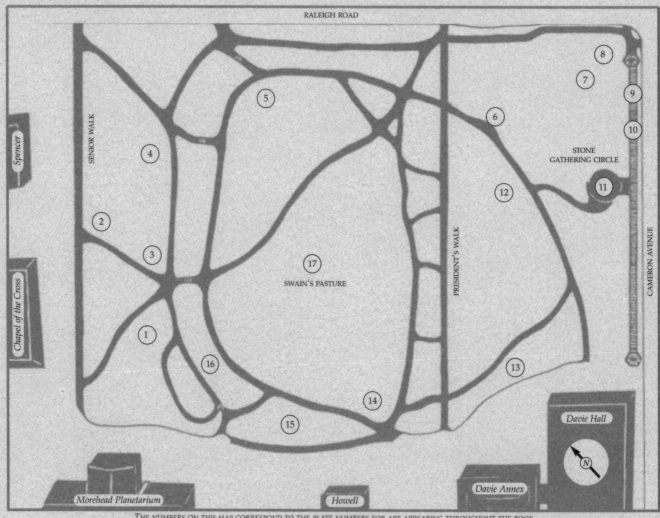

RALEIGH ROAD

Spencer

SENIOR WALK

Chapel of the Cross

⑧

⑦

⑨

⑩

STONE
GATHERING CIRCLE

⑪

CAMERON AVENUE

⑤

④

⑥

⑫

②

③

⑰

SWAIN'S PASTURE

PRESIDENT'S WALK

①

⑬

⑯

⑭

Davie Hall

⑮

N

Morehead Planetarium

Howell

Davie Annex

THE NUMBERS ON THIS MAP CORRESPOND TO THE PLATE NUMBERS FOR ART APPEARING THROUGHOUT THE BOOK

① MORNING—ARBORETUM—1903

② WALTER'S PINE

③ MARSHALL'S HAWTHORN

④ BALD CYPRESS AND RED MAPLE

⑤ ARB TRIO

⑥ INCENSE CEDAR AND JAPANESE MAPLE

⑦ EASTERN HEMLOCK

⑧ LONG-LEAF PINE

⑨ UNDER THE ARBOR

⑩ CROSSVINE AND WISTERIA

⑪ SPRING—COKER ARBORETUM

⑫ WITCH'S BROOM

⑬ ROUND-LOBED SWEET-GUM

⑭ BEE TREE

⑮ COKER ARBORETUM MAGNOLIAS

⑯ LYCORIS

⑰ MORNING IN THE ARBORETUM [2003]

PLATE 1 *Beverly Dixon*   *MORNING - ARBORETUM - 1903*   *Oil*

In the early twentieth century, five acres marking the eastern edge of campus were a boggy meadow, unfit to build upon and inhabited by only a few willows and black gum trees. The meadow was referred to as Swain's Pasture for former University of North Carolina president David L. Swain, who, like many of the faculty, grazed his livestock here.

Old Cuddy, the president's cow, spent many an afternoon pasturing in the meadow. The arbor that forms the southern border of the Arboretum today appears in the background of the painting.

In 1903, University president Francis Venable asked Dr. William Chambers Coker, the University of North Carolina's first professor of botany and the first chairman of the Buildings and Grounds Committee, to beautify Swain's Pasture. With an appropriation of $10 and one gardener, Dr. Coker began the process of transforming the bog into a magnificent arboretum. Coker once stated in a letter, "We Americans have been very negligent in our failure to propagate the best varieties of our own highly ornamental native plants." With this in mind, he began to turn these five acres into a showcase that would feature the trees and shrubs of the southeastern United States and serve as an outdoor classroom for students of botany.

DR. WILLIAM CHAMBERS COKER
Photo by J. Horton

In the beginning, Dr. Coker worked on the most elevated ground in the Arboretum's northwest corner, planting specimens such as the Walter's pine, *Pinus glabra*, which has a limited range along the eastern coast from South Carolina to Florida. Planted in 1920, this tree has grown to be the world's best specimen of the species. In 1992, having attained a height of 98 feet and a circumference of 137 inches, it won the distinction of State Champion. A perfect balance of mass and grace, its lichen-covered trunk gives rise to an impressive canopy, which has become a favorite nesting spot for red-tailed hawks.

Standing next to the Senior Walk, which runs along the northern end of the Arboretum, this magnificent tree has been a silent witness to thousands of students as they marched toward commencement. Perhaps it is also the most romantic tree in the Arboretum—numerous couples have picnicked in its shade, and some have chosen to exchange their wedding vows beneath its boughs.

PLATE 2 *Natalie Crawford* WALTER'S PINE *Acrylic*

Just beneath the Walter's pine is the Marshall's hawthorn, *Crataegus marshallii*, "the prettiest thing in the Arboretum," according to Dr. Coker. Indeed a tree for all seasons, the hawthorn's mottled bark and sinewy limbs provide winter interest, while its white flowers, dissected leaves, and bright red fruits enchant the garden during spring, summer, and fall. Cardinals, often thick amongst its branches in the autumn, eat its ripened fruit.

PLATE 3 *Dorothy Wilbur-Brooks*   *MARSHALL'S HAWTHORN*   *Watercolor*

The old hawthorn blew over in a storm many years ago, and its branches took root where they lay in the soil, giving it an unusually broad form. In celebration of the Arboretum's 100th birthday in April 2003, and in honor of Dr. Coker's esteem for the tree, we planted a young Marshall's hawthorn where the old one originally stood.

Nearby, the bald cypress, *Taxodium distichum*, and eastern red maple, *Acer rubrum*, speak to Dr. Coker's genius in site-appropriate planting. Having identified this area as perennially moist, he chose trees that would thrive in such conditions.

Cypress trees frequently develop a wide base with gnarly protrusions, called "knees," which serve to anchor the tree in soft soil and may help provide oxygen to the submerged roots.

Both the bald cypress and the red maple transform their appearance over the seasons. The red maple, one of the first plants to flower each year, sends out its crimson buds to glow against the late winter sky. Then as spring comes, the lime-green needles of the cypress emerge, lending a feathery texture to the garden.

In summer, you might see a squirrel rappelling down the trunk of the cypress, biting off a strip of bark to use for construction of a nest nearby. Come autumn, the maple's leaves range in color from deep red to brilliant yellow; and the cypress, having turned a radiant amber, fills the sky with warmth in the afternoon sun.

PLATE 4 *Kristen Dill* BALD CYPRESS AND RED MAPLE *Watercolor*

A slender tree with smooth, grayish bark, *Camptotheca acuminata* (depicted in the upper left) is a deciduous species from China that has been the object of much interest of late, because it contains a potent anti-cancer compound, Camptothecin™, in its bark and wood. Scientists at North Carolina's Research Triangle Institute began testing the compound's properties in the early 1960s and, in the mid-1990s, successfully created two synthetic versions, topotecan and irinotecan, for treatment in breast, colon, ovarian, and lung cancers.

The Arboretum also contains a number of other medical plants. The Japanese plum-yew, *Cephalotaxus harringtonia* (depicted in the lower left), has roots that contain a compound, homoharrintonine, which has proven to be effective in treating certain kinds of leukemia. *Ginkgo biloba* (on the right), easily recognized by its fan-shaped leaves which turn a brilliant yellow in autumn, has been used as an herbal supplement to improve memory. Male ginkgo trees are commonly used in landscaping because the female trees produce seeds with a fleshy covering that has an unpleasant odor. Known from fossils 225 million years old, gingko is an ancient tree that once grew all over the world. Over eons, its worldwide distribution dwindled until there were only a few small populations in Asia. Many now believe the ginkgo was saved from extinction because of its sacred place in the culture of China, where it has been planted around temples for centuries.

Medicinal botany is one of the garden's oldest themes. In 1915, Henry Roland Totten, a former student of Dr. Coker and specialist in pharmaceutical botany, joined the Arboretum founder in developing the site. With plans to start a drug garden in the southwestern corner of the Arboretum, the two men began procuring seeds and rootstock of plants used in medicines. In the early twentieth century, such plants were essential to medical practice. Indeed, their scarcity during those World War I years (1914–1919) was bringing much attention to their importance. By 1925, the drug garden, one-fifth of an acre in size, contained 176 species. Today, this spirit of interpreting the medicinal values of plants lives on in the Mercer Reeves Hubbard Herb Garden at the North Carolina Botanical Garden's main visitor site on the U.S. 15-501 Bypass and Old Mason Farm Road.

PLATE 5 *Marriott Little*   *ARB TRIO*   *Acrylic*

STUDENTS ENJOYING COKER ARBORETUM

Photo by Diane Birkemo

Alongside its history as an outdoor classroom, the Arboretum has had a longstanding reputation as one of the best places on campus for relaxation. On pleasant days throughout the years, students and visitors have enjoyed quietude on one of the many garden benches, sat on a blanket in the sunlight, or played games on the lawn. Such times have forged a bond between the Arboretum and generations of alumni, who have fond memories of spending time here.

AUTUMN UMBRELLA (OVERLAY)   *Photo by Daniel Stern*

KEMP NYE, 1934   *Photo from University Alumni Report / GAA Files*

In the mid-1930s, UNC student Kemp Nye created one such memory when he swung, Tarzan-like, from tree to tree across the Arboretum. Nye, who began studying at the University in 1934, lived in Grimes Hall and was very familiar with the Arboretum across the street from his dormitory.

Perhaps inspired by Johnny Weismuller, the Olympic swimmer who became famous as the title character in the film *Tarzan of the Apes*, Kemp Nye wagered with some classmates that he could cross the Arboretum without touching the ground. The bet promised the winner a week of lunches, each to consist of a sandwich and chocolate milk.

On the appointed day, Nye climbed into a tree near Davie Hall, zigzagged across the Arboretum, and emerged 22 minutes later at the rear of Spencer Hall, victorious and looking forward to a week's free lunches.

In addition to the gingko, the Arboretum boasts another "living fossil" in the dawn redwood, *Metasequoia glyptostroboides*, a species that was thought to be extinct until 1946, when a Chinese botanist discovered an isolated population in the Szechwan Province of his country. In 1948, Boston's Arnold Arboretum sent a team to the Szechwan to collect seeds, which were then grown out and distributed to botanical institutions. Our dawn redwood, planted in 1950, was one of those distributed by the Arnold Arboretum.

Near the President's Walk stands a group of plants that demonstrate some of the ways that nature shapes a garden. For example, the common buttonbush, *Cephalanthus occidentalis*, was struck by neighboring trees during Hurricane Fran in 1996. Heavily damaged, the plant was cut to the ground and allowed to re-sprout from its base, resulting in a much more compact and ornamental habit than is typical for the species. The graceful, arching trunk nearby belongs to a California incense-cedar, *Calocedrus decurrens*, native to California, Oregon, and Nevada. Blown askew during its early years, this tree was cabled to the ground and subsequently took on the dramatic form you see in the painting. The trunk, riddled with tiny holes that were created by yellow-bellied sapsuckers, continually seeps resin. And opposite the incense cedar stands a broad Japanese maple, *Acer palmatum* 'Tamukeyama,' whose umbrella-like form gradually encroached upon the original path edge. Rather than prune the plant unevenly, we widened the path to accommodate the shape of this beautiful specimen. Beneath the tree's dense canopy lies a terrific hiding place for some garden residents, such as the eastern cottontail rabbit, which in summer likes to dart out and snack on nearby flowering annuals.

PLATE 6 *Sally Sutton*   *INCENSE CEDAR AND JAPANESE MAPLE*   *Oil*

In addition to his interest in medicinal drug plants, Dr. Totten was very fond of conifers. He planted many of the Arboretum's older ones, such as the long-leaf pine from the southeastern Coastal Plain and the eastern hemlock from the southern Appalachian mountains, thereby creating an interesting juxtaposition of native conifers with very different natural ranges.

PLATE 7 *Katherine Shelburne*   *EASTERN HEMLOCK*   *Watercolor*

With its graceful, sweeping branches and dark green needles, eastern hemlock, *Tsuga canadensis*, is considered a "climax" tree in southern Appalachia, because its shade is so dense that little else can grow beneath it. Sadly, infestations of an introduced insect, the hemlock wooly adelgid, now severely threaten hemlocks from New England to the Southeast.

PLATE 8 *Katherine Shelburne*   LONG-LEAF PINE   *Watercolor*

Long-leaf pine, *Pinus palustris*, is a coastal plain tree that ranges from Virginia to Florida and west to Texas. Its long needles, which may grow up to 18 inches, and large cones make this pine easily recognizable in the wild. This tree has a unique appearance in youth during its "grass stage," when bundles of needles appear from the base before any trunk is formed. The sticky sap of the long-leaf pine was a major source for the turpentine, pitch, and tar industries in the mid-1800s.

Built in 1911, the original arbor structure was funded by a $100 donation from a Mrs. Shipp in honor of her father and uncle. Its timbers were logs of black locust, *Robinia psuedoacacia*. Arbor plantings at that time included Carolina jessamine, *Gelsemium sempervirens*, and three species of wisteria. Over time, one of these species—Chinese wisteria, *Wisteria sinensis*—proved to be invasive and monopolized the arbor. During the renovation of the arbor in 1996-97, Arboretum staff removed the invasive vines and replanted with native alternatives.

On the southeastern corner of the Arboretum stands a small stone pedestal bearing a plaque in honor of Dr. Coker, presented by the Class of 1967.

The arbor is now a prominent display of more than a dozen native flowering vines—including American wisteria, *Wisteria frutescens*, and crossvine, *Bignonia capreolata*, depicted below—that provide diversity and interest year-round.

PLATE 10   *Dorothy Wilbur-Brooks*
CROSSVINE AND WISTERIA
Watercolor

Notice how all the wisteria vines twist counter-clockwise as they grow upward. The direction of growth in climbing plants, called circumnutation, varies from species to species.

PLATE 9 *Pamela Pease*   UNDER THE ARBOR   *Pop-up Paper Sculpture*

The stone gathering circle was created as part of the arbor renovation and is a memorial gift from the University of North Carolina at Chapel Hill's Class of 1997. As you approach the circle, take note of the plaque that honors students in this class who died in the tragic fraternity fire of May 1996 and other classmates who did not survive to graduate.

The gathering circle is an serves as a focal point for groups. The seat-level this area's use by reaffirming Dr. Coker's Arboretum function room. Indeed, classes disciplines, ranging the arts, use the space.

entry to the garden and tours and activity stonewall facilitates University students, dream to have the as an outdoor class- in many different from life sciences to

TULIP POPLAR MOSAIC
Photo by Rob Gardner

In the center of the gathering circle is a large mosaic leaf of a tulip poplar, *Liriodendron tulipifera*, also known as the tulip-tree. The midvein of the leaf points toward the campus's ancient Davie Poplar. Legend tells us that in 1792 a committee looking for a site for the proposed university picnicked under the boughs of the magnificent poplar that was later named in honor of William R. Davie, who had lobbied in favor of legislation to create the University of North Carolina.

PLATE 11 *Patricia Mae Young*   *SPRING—COKER ARBORETUM*   *Pastel*

PLATE 12A *Tama Hochbaum*   WITCH'S BROOM   *Photo Collage*

Down the path stands the large loblolly pine, *Pinus taeda*, which has an unusual growth about 50 feet up on the far side of the tree. This dense formation of branches, called a witch's broom, is caused when an insect or disease penetrates the bark. The result is repeated dieback on the infected branch, causing a very compact form.

Although witch's brooms can be harmful to trees, this one has proven to be benign. Its round shape has remained about the same size for years. In fact, many horticulturists prize the compact habit of these unusual growths and, through seed-collection and cuttings, try to propagate them and create new varieties of ornamental plants. One such clone, which was produced from this witch's broom, currently resides in the Arboretum and has matured into a novel dwarf loblolly with a gnarled and dense habit.

PLATE 12B *Tama Hochbaum* WITCH'S BROOM *Photo Collage*

The typical form of sweet-gum has star-shaped leaves and produces a spike-covered fruit. Many people object to having their lawn littered every year by these "gum-balls," so the round-lobed variety, *Liquidambar styraciflua* var. *rotundiloba*, which does not produce them, has become increasingly popular in the landscape trade.

I recently received a phone call from a woman in Pinehurst, North Carolina, introducing herself as the daughter of Mr. R.E. Wicker, who discovered this unusual form of sweet-gum in 1930. She said, "My Daddy gave that tree to Dr. Coker because he thought the Arboretum should have one." She went on to describe the area near Pinehurst where Mr. Wicker found the original plant, and commented that it has since died. We are allowing a sucker sprout of the round-lobed sweet-gum to mature, ensuring that another generation of this special tree will be part of the Arboretum.

PLATE 13 *Emma Skurnick*　　　ROUND-LOBED SWEET-GUM　　　*Mixed Media*

STONE CULVERT   *Photo by Daniel Stern*

Completed in 1907, the culvert running through the middle of the garden is an example of the masonry work that has been an essential part of the Coker Arboretum from the beginning. Much of the first decade's efforts went toward the installation of an elaborate system of sub-surface drainage tile that made the soil more suitable for trees and shrubs. Although precise maps from that time period are sparse, records show that more than a mile of such drainage was installed.

Rising amidst a hedge of sweet breath of spring, *Lonicera fragrantissima*, is an old black locust, *Robinia pseudoacacia*, that was struck by lightning many years ago. Despite being hollow, the tree remains standing, a living testimony to the wood's resistance to decay.

One popular saying about black locust wood is that it "lasts a few years longer than stone." It is for this reason that black locust has, for many generations, been a favorite in the construction of split-rail fences and structures like the arbor.

Our hollow black locust has also become a habitat tree, hosting several different life forms, including a colony of wild honeybees that took up residence in the tree several years ago. The honeybees venture out into the garden all summer long to collect pollen from our many flowers. If left undisturbed, the wild honeybees keep to themselves.

PLATE 14 *Jennifer E. Miller*   BEE TREE   *Acrylic*

PLATE 15 *Barb Spang* COKER ARBORETUM MAGNOLIAS *Pastel*

Dr. Coker's promenade of old southern magnolias, *Magnolia grandiflora*, creates a buffer between the garden and the hustle and bustle of campus. The trees' massive trunks and glossy evergreen leaves are brightened each summer by the thick, fragrant petals of their large, white blossoms. Planted nearby are some other magnolia species that lose their leaves each fall, such as the shrubby star magnolia, *Magnolia stellata*, from Asia, which is covered with showy white flowers in the early spring before the new leaves emerge. The juxtaposition of these magnolia species speaks to the phenomenon of vicariance, an evolutionary process occurring in some species in widely separated geographical areas that are descended from common ancestors.

Millions of years ago, plants living on the super-continent of Laurasia were separated as the earth's tectonic plates shifted to create North America and Eurasia. Remarkably, some widely separated geographic areas, like eastern North America and eastern Asia, share important climatic conditions. Dr. Coker commented on the similarities between the flora of these regions, noting "a type of vegetation corresponding in families and even genera with a similar extension from the north downward in eastern Asia." The Arboretum has grown to include specimens of families like the magnolias, which illustrate the unique vicariant relationship between our flora and that of Asia.

PLATE 16 *Dorothy Wilbur-Brooks*   *LYCORIS*   *Watercolor*

The fall-blooming spider lily, *Lycoris radiata*, an unusual bulb from Asia, occurs throughout the garden. The plant sends up a bare stalk in late summer that is soon topped with a delicate red blossom. After flowering, strap-like leaves emerge in large clumps from around the stem's base and remain through winter and well into spring before going dormant again. Coker wrote, "One of the most successful bulbs we have tested in the Arboretum is the spider lily . . . Extensive beds and borders of it give us our most brilliant display of the whole year." The variety of this plant that we have in the Arboretum possesses uncommonly large flowers. It was only readily available in commerce prior to World War II, when trade lines to Asia became restricted.

PLATE 17 *Margaret Brunson Hill*   *MORNING IN THE ARBORETUM [2003]*   *Oil*

The magnificent sweet-gum, *Liquidambar styraciflua*, was planted in the open central lawn and, without the competition of neighbors, has had plenty of sunlight. As a result, it has developed an unusually broad form with many large lower limbs. Each fall it puts on a magnificent display as the leaves change to colors ranging from deep purple to blazing orange. In the background of the painting, notice the trunk of a huge overcup oak, *Quercus lyrata*, one of the oldest trees in the Arboretum, and beneath the limbs of the old oak, a man taking his dog on their daily walk.

WEDDING ON THE LAWN, 1955

Photo by T.A. Redmon, courtesy of Ben and Margaret Williams

The central lawn area, framed by magnificent trees, is frequented by students looking for a place to study or relax on pleasant days throughout the year and used by groups doing outdoor theater, tai chi, and music. This sun-dappled lawn also provides a beautiful environment for wedding ceremonies and is the site of some of the most treasured memories carried in the hearts of those who have enjoyed this garden haven throughout its 100-year history.

WHO BUILT THIS PLACE?
A poem commemorating the Coker Arboretum Centennial
J.R. Massey, Herbarium Curator Emeritus, North Carolina Botanical Garden

In shade or sun, in quiet or busy
we read, study, relax, meditate, and even play
in this special place.
In beauty, we nurture our minds, spirit and bodies.
Who built this place?

From the age of these trees and paths
it is clear that this place was conceived long ago.
To whom do we owe the thanks for the idea and the labor
to build a place like this in the hustle and bustle of a campus and town?
A space so grand that visitors who attended these colleges and halls return over and over
to this place.
Some married here,
many have laughed and cried here
and sadly some have died here.
This is hallowed ground.

Long a laboratory for students and visitors
it is a living museum of rare and beautiful, of antique and common
of useful and of endangered plants that entreats our minds.
Some who may never tramp forests and fields
bogs, swamps, and pocosins
because of opportunity, age or disability
who might never see a magnificent specimen,
or touch or smell it, or gaze and wonder at it
can do so here!
Who built this place?

A painter, writer, or poet finds inspiration
That elusive equation or algorithm comes easily and quietly to mind.
Still others find peace or just respite from workaday affairs.
Who built and nurtured this place
where creative seeds germinate
and spirits are refreshed?

Rumor or history says this was once a low
pasture where milch cows grazed
and nourished the faculty and students
of a budding university.

If we close our eyes
perhaps we see a brown Swiss or Guernsey nursing her calf.
Perhaps if we listen, we can hear the footsteps and voices
of students heading to war
or better yet returning.

Or perhaps it is the footfalls or the clink of spades of our botanical mentors.
Of Dr. Coker who conceived and planned this place
of Drs. Totten and Couch, or Miss Alma and Preacher,
of Olive, Bell, and Parks or Jones, Brooks, Birkemo, Presler and so recently Stern.
Each has left their special footprint and mark on this glorious place.

This venerable collection stands today
survivor of hurricanes, tornadoes, floods, beetles and pollution
of budget shortfalls and wars,
of horticultural and botanical trends and fads,
of pressures of town and campus sprawl.
It is a living tribute to all those who have
made this a special place in their minds, hearts
and through their plans and actions.
A place preserved by vision, and action, over the past century.

May we on this occasion reaffirm our commitment
to perpetuate this place and collections!
Let us underscore the value of this place to education, to art, beauty, and health
As a botanical treasure, an icon of our respect for nature,
a monument to the rich and precious natural history of our region and state!
May the spirit of our recognition and support today
and our deeds in the days to come
mingle amongst even older and stately trees and this lovely green space
at the celebration of the Coker Arboretum's Bicentennial
With those in attendance again raising the question of who has built and preserved this wondrous place
and each answering then as now
you can count on me!

Appendix

COMMON NAME	SCIENTIFIC NAME	DISTRIBUTION
* Eastern Red Maple	*Acer rubrum*	Eastern North America
Japanese Maple	*Acer palmatum 'Tamukeyama'*	China, Korea, and Japan
Japanese Maple	*Acer palmatum 'Dissectum'*	China, Korea, and Japan
* Cross-vine	*Bignonia capreolata*	Southeastern United States
California Incense-cedar	*Calocedrus decurrens*	Nevada, Oregon, and California
Camptotheca	*Camptotheca acuminata*	China
* Common Buttonbush	*Cephalanthus occidentalis*	Eastern North America
Japanese Plum-yew	*Cephalotaxus harringtonia*	Japan
* Marshall's Hawthorn	*Crataegus marshallii*	Southeastern United States
* Carolina Jessamine	*Gelsemium sempervirens*	Southeastern United States and Mexico
Ginkgo	*Ginkgo biloba*	Southeastern China
* Sweet-gum	*Liquidambar styraciflua*	Eastern United States and Guatemala
* Round-leaf Sweet-gum	*Liquidambar styraciflua* var. *rotundiloba*	North Carolina
* Tulip Poplar or Tulip-tree	*Liriodendron tulipifera*	Eastern North America
Sweet Breath of Spring	*Lonicera fragrantissima*	Eastern China
Spider Lily or Magic-Lily	*Lycoris radiata*	China
* Southern Magnolia	*Magnolia grandiflora*	Southeastern United States
Star Magnolia	*Magnolia stellata*	Japan
Dawn Redwood	*Metasequoia glyptostroboides*	Western China
* Walter's Pine	*Pinus glabra*	Southeastern United States
* Long-leaf Pine	*Pinus palustris*	Southeastern United States
* Loblolly Pine	*Pinus taeda*	Southeastern United States
* Overcup Oak	*Quercus lyrata*	Eastern United States
* Black Locust	*Robinia psuedoacacia*	Eastern and central United States
* Bald-cypress	*Taxodium distichum*	Eastern United States
* Eastern Hemlock	*Tsuga canadensis*	Eastern North America
* American Wisteria	*Wisteria frutescens*	Southeastern United States
Chinese Wisteria	*Wisteria sinensis*	China

*Indicates native species that are defined here as plants occurring other than as a result of an introduction within a twelve-state region of the southeastern United States (from the Mississippi River to the Atlantic Ocean and from the Gulf of Mexico north to Kentucky, West Virginia, Maryland, and Delaware.)